The Romance of Hats

THE ROMANCE OF
Hats

The Editors of *Victoria* Magazine
Foreword by Nancy Lindemeyer

HEARST BOOKS
New York

Library of Congress Cataloging-in-Publication Data

Victoria: the romance of hats.

p. cm.

By the editors of Victoria magazine.

ISBN 0-688-12636-7

1. Hats. 2. Millinery. I. Victoria (New York, N.Y.).

TT657.V53   1994

391'.43 ~ dc20   93-5641

CIP

PRINTED IN ITALY by ARTI GRAFICHE RICORDI S.p.A. - MILAN

First Edition

1 2 3 4 5 6 7 8 9 10

For Victoria ~
Nancy Lindemeyer, Editor-in-Chief
Bryan E. McCay, Art Director
John Mack Carter, Director, Magazine Development

Edited by Laurie Orseck
Designed by Nina Ovryn
Jacket design by Bryan E. McCay
Text by Jeanine Larmoth
Produced by Smallwood and Stewart, Inc., New York City

Contents

⊼

Foreword

⟨symbol⟩

*D*oes anyone still wear a hat?"
inquires songwriter Stephen Sondheim in his witty lyrics for "The
Ladies Who Lunch." If there is any doubt, we are here with *The
Romance of Hats* to state emphatically that not only do women
today still wear hats, they buy them, they create them ~ and their
interest in them grows stronger every day.

For me, hats have always been a way to change my personality in
an instant. If I want to be a countess, a hat will provide me with exactly
the right prop to begin my imaginings. A flower girl? An Eliza Doolittle
straw hat will take me to Covent Garden. Hats have the power to trans-
port us to other times and places and personas as well as keeping us
warm and making us beautiful on all the most important occasions. In
this book there are dozens to try on and dozens to inspire your next
shopping trip. I hope you enjoy *The Romance of Hats,* and I especially
hope it inspires you to don one of your own and sally forth feeling fabu-
lous. And yes, Mr. Sondheim, women still do wear hats.

Nancy Lindemeyer
Editor-in-Chief, *Victoria* Magazine

I

A LOVE AFFAIR
WITH HATS

I CONSIDER

THAT WITHOUT HATS, AN

INTRINSIC PART OF

FASHION, WE WOULD HAVE

NO CIVILIZATION.

Christian Dior

e have always been faithful to hats. They are valentines, tributes to the femininity of little girls, young girls, women, a perennial delight to wear. A hat is a shameless flatterer, calling attention to an escaping curl, a tawny braid, a sprinkling of freckles over a pert nose, directing the eye to what is most unique about a face. Its curves emphasize a shining pair of eyes, a lofty forehead; its deep brim accentuates the pale tint of a cheek, creates an aura of prettiness, suggests a mystery that awakens curiosity in the onlooker.

A hat is, after all, a crown, a crown that can make any woman, as she places one on her head, feel set apart, queenly. It matters little whether it is hardly more than a circlet of flowers or as impressive as a lofty toque. With a hat, a woman accepts the invitation to become a poet. Because hats, like all fashion, are a means of self-expression, the most memorable are far more than simple utilitarian coverings for the

The sepia-tinted vintage rose, above, with
surrounding leaves of velvet and sprigs of forget-me-nots,
is ready to make a hat blossom. The white straw, opposite,
is twined with gauzy flowers and a wisp of tulle.

head, practical shelters from sun and wind, something to get us through an occasion and then be pushed to the back of a shelf. The best-designed hats are bold, they amuse, they impose, they challenge, they mimic, they intrigue, they recapture some spirit of the past, predict some wave of the future. They are works of art.

Hats have always been treated with a special reverence. From their perches in shops and department stores, they seem to beckon to passersby with a curving ostrich feather, perhaps, a paving of black sequins, a scalloping of felt, a dipping brim that recalls a languid lady in a Gainsborough painting. Few women have ever been able to ignore so delicious a summons. Few have been able to resist the temptation to try on a hat and discover in the mirror a person they never suspected was there. A hat alters the image we have of ourselves, and the image others

*A velvety heroine's hat, above, boasts a brim
swept down in back as deeply as a sea captain's sou'wester.
Opposite, a proud black hat with curling feather from Patina
suggests the boldness of the buccaneer.*

see as well. For the hours we wear it, it brings out different dimensions in our personality, much as a costume aids an actress in her role.

Because a hat can so powerfully effect an image, it can become an intrinsic part of it. Who can think of Queen Elizabeth's grandmother, Queen Mary, without the toque that rose in a great pile, sprouting an aigrette, over her marcelled waves of silver hair and ramrod-straight back? Her toque was long out of fashion, but she was unconcerned. The queen didn't ignore fashion, she transcended it. Other famous women are similarly identified with their hats: Danish writer Isak Dinesen, her winding turban accentuating her enormous, burning eyes; Virginia

*Thomas Hardy's Tess of the D'Urbervilles might
have chosen the straw gardening hat, left, tied with a lace
fichu. Above, the cloche, the ultimate twenties shape, recalls
the piquant chic of F. Scott Fitzgerald's Great Gatsby.*

Woolf, haloed by a gardening hat that softened her austere features;
Jacqueline Kennedy, the President's wife, in a pillbox that was her ges-
ture to the correctness expected in the early sixties.

Some of our favorite literary heroines ~ often portrayed on the
screen as well ~ appear before the mind's eye in familiar hats: Scarlett
O'Hara, undoubted mistress of Margaret Mitchell's epic *Gone with the
Wind,* runs half floating in her hoopskirts over the lawn of her adored
family home, Tara, in a sweeping leghorn straw tied on with green velvet
streamers. Charlotte Brontë's Jane Eyre reveals her character and her past
in the straw bonnet and shawl that are the insignia of her childhood at a
charity school. The little band of girls that figures so prominently in

Ruffled roses made of French ribbons cast a glow on an open-weave straw hat by Louise Green, above left. Above right, a black felt riding hat from Kokin would suit Tolstoy's Anna Karenina.

Marcel Proust's *Remembrance of Things Past* strolls at the seaside clinging to natty boaters. Jane Austen's young ladies, holding frilly parasols to shade their eyes and high-crowned bonnets from the sun, step off the pages of her novels. Colette's Gigi can never be other than an innocent and irresistible child-woman in her full-blown sailor hat.

Our sense of historical figures often follows the same path. The most ravishing beauty the world has known, the Egyptian queen Nefertiti, would be but half a queen without her stately *tahj*, a flattened cone raised high above her perfect forehead. The tragic destiny awaiting Mary, Queen of Scots, seems almost foretold by the heart-shaped black velvet cap rimmed in pearls that cupped her face as if it were a treasure.

*A platter of petals, above left, is
whisked over with an enveloping pink haze.
Above right, just such a plush outsize
sailor hat might have been glimpsed in
Henry James's New York City.*

If, as the saying goes, clothes make the man, it might also be said that hats make the woman. Over the centuries and over the world, hats have provided a quicker way than clothes to identify a woman ~ as chic, as daring, as up-to-date, as old-fashioned, as romantic. Hats have been retreats for the modest and accessories to sauciness. They have revealed the wearer's attitude, if only by hiding it. They have also spelled out who the woman was, her importance or lack of it, her place in society. In simplest terms, this has often meant that the more extravagant, impractical, or uncomfortable the hat, the higher the woman's rank. In the Middle Ages, only ladies wore the tall, cone-shaped hennin, its veil fluttering like a standard above a castle tower, or the wimple, which enclosed the head

HAT PINS

Like long icicles glistening with jewels faux or real, filigreed metal, and etched crystal, hat pins came into their own at the turn of the century. Hats had exploded into almost insupportable spectacles of stuffed birds, flowers, and veils. And they were to be worn everywhere: visiting, motoring, at the theater in the afternoon, even at home. Creations so monumental required safe anchorage. Hat pins ensured that even if the car went as fast as fifteen miles an hour, or if the wearer went wild applauding a matinee performance, the hat would remain immobile and glorious. In the twenties, hat pins found themselves on the crest of the costume jewelry wave, in materials as dissimilar as celluloid and coral. Today the hat pin, for too long an object prized by collectors only, is once again a practical treasure.

In a portrait from 1900, the Edwardian sailor hat, above, piled high with cabbage roses, lends its wearer the charm of a literary heroine. Right, treasured vintage flowers adorn a new hat with the poetry of the past.

and surrounded the face in starchy linen. A peasant girl could never have dreamt of such agonizing delights. Though a lady might adopt the hat of a shepherdess or a milkmaid to amuse herself, as Marie Antoinette did, there was no possibility of its happening the other way around.

According to Alison Lurie in *The Language of Clothes*, ladies' hats have also indicated their social roles. Throughout most of the nineteenth century, the respectable woman, whether wife, widow, or spinster, wore not one but two head coverings. From sunup to sundown, the lady cloistered her head in a muslin or silk cap, trimmed with ribbon or lace. Evening parties were the only times she

was permitted to appear in public bareheaded.

Until the 1950s hats were still a "must" for ladies, whether lunching together in the city, attending business or club meetings, playing bridge, or going to church. Then came the sixties, when for the first time in history, the woman's hat ceased to distinguish class, time, or place; in fact, the hat virtually ceased to be. Fortunately, after an almost twelve-year absence from the social and fashion scene, the hat returned to favor in the late 1970s. Rather than stifling a woman, as it often had before, and showing she "knew her place," the hat became a means to self-invention.

By now, the hat's past has become a cupboard for all to dip into, a witty historical reference book to quote from, a means of retrieving the moods of the past. A soft cloche may call up an image of the steam-swathed platform of the luxurious Orient Express in the twenties, its compartments crammed with the titled; the jaunty straw sailor may bring to mind a turn-of-the-century Gibson girl lobbing tennis balls over the net; a flower-trimmed straw may evoke the smiles and good manners of a garden party in an English village.

Melinda Hodges has created two variations on the Edwardian toque: on the left a classic silhouette in pearlescent strawberry-pink satin, and on the right a sassier version, with a dropped crown in oatmeal linen and black taffeta.

For
Safekeeping

⌖

It is possible that hats are just an excuse to gather together a splendid assortment of hatboxes. Yet for all its apparent frivolity ~ the prettily patterned paper or sprigged chintz covering it ~ a hatbox is actually the best way to store and protect hats. Such enemies as dust, light, and moisture are kept at bay, perhaps aided by a bag of lavender-scented moth crystals. A hatbox also brings order to the closet ~ a worthy function in itself.

To best preserve them in their boxes, hats with upturned brims should be laid flat; those with downturned brims should be floated on a ball of crumpled tissue paper stuffed in the crown. (Ideally, all should be swathed in acid-free paper.) No hat should ever be stored upside down or crowded next to anything else.

II

ELEMENTS OF A HAT

here are few shapes a hat can take. For this reason, most silhouettes come round again and again ~ scaled down, blown up, in other fabrics, with other trims, set at different angles, balancing other figures, flattering other faces, playing different roles. One hat may dominate for a time, then another, leaving an old friend behind. But the forgotten hat is always there, waiting to make its triumphant return. "The only new things in the world are the forgotten ones," said Marie Antoinette's milliner, Rose Bertin, two centuries ago.

The cushiony toque, something like a soft stovepipe hat that has been sat on ~ all the rage before the First World War ~ reappeared in this decade in a smaller version. The fisherman's sou'wester was brought ashore in the fifties, when designer Elsa Schiaparelli angled its collar-covering brim in back, replaced the cheery yellow with bold black, and turned it into high fashion. Even silhouettes as curious as the tall cone-shaped tutulus of the ancient Etruscans and the Phrygian stocking cap

*A deep-crowned, mushroom-colored felt
hat designed by Tia Mazza, above and opposite, wreathed
in a wild gathering of flowers, vines, and leaves in winey
hues, echoes the Edwardian silhouette.*

that marked the freed slave in Greece have had repeated chances at pop-ularity. The tutulus came back in the Middle Ages as the hennin; in 1939, the hennin was back, covered in printed silk by Schiaparelli. The Phrygian cap returned to distinguish the doges who ruled Venice during the Renaissance, then the French revolutionaries.

The following are among the favorite silhouettes that have proved their greatness and wearability by frequent returns to fashion prominence.

The Turban. Almost five thousand years ago, Mesopotamian women were wrapping their heads in the intricate folds of the turban. Women have been doing so ever since. It's no wonder, for with no more than a length of supple cloth and deft fingers, a woman can fashion a hat that is both practical and handsome. Whenever a taste for the exotic

takes over fashion, the turban seems to be the first hat to make a reappearance. In 1913, with the world in the grip of tango fever, women got in the mood by slithering into dresses draped and split in front, and tugging aigrette-flourishing turbans down over their eyebrows.

The Boater. Also called the sailor, this flat-topped round hat of straw is usually encircled by a ribbon. As its name indicates, it owes its origins to sailors and the sea. Admiral Horatio Nelson, the hero of the battle of Trafalgar in 1805, first made a hard, round straw hat part of the regulation dress for his crews. Boaters are still part of the uniform at older public schools in England. In 1870, a machine for sewing straw brought the boater into the mainstream; since that time, they have been worn, slightly cocked, by debonaire men strolling city streets in summer; on the back of the head by sailor-jacketed boys and girls at boat ponds; and tipped over the noses of dashing young ladies.

The Beret. A round, soft cap, the beret was worn by Etruscan huntsmen around the fifth century B.C. Its simplicity and practicality have made it one of the most widely worn hats in the world, especially by men who work out of doors, by artists, and by the military. Rain, snow, and dust won't harm it, and it can easily be stowed in a pocket. Women adopted the beret during the Second World War; for them, it is, if anything, more useful than it is for a man. As a head covering, it not only protects, it conceals the hair when it is "not at its best." Its suppleness also allows women to tug it this way and that, even putting it, as little girls do, on the back of the head, until they achieve the most becoming angle.

*For the belle of the Orient Express or
the Train Bleu: The head-hugging curves of a bell-
shaped cloche with a bee-stung brim are accentuated
by a dizzy swirl of chocolate stripes.*

The classical gentleman's bowler, above, is delicately
tailored in gray felt with a silken encrusting of lace. Opposite,
a felt cloche in its pre-twenties form, its large soft brim giving
only a tantalizing glimpse of the eyes.

The Cloche. A head-hugging hat shaped like a bell (*cloche* means
"bell" in French), the cloche is considered a hallmark of the twenties, an
indispensable element of the flapper's wardrobe. French milliners were
famous for cutting and shaping the cloche to suit each customer's face. In
the thirties, legendary actress Greta Garbo pushed a felt cloche back from
her forehead, revealing her magnificent eyes, and the slouch was born.

The Pillbox. One step up from the crown-covering skullcap and
two steps down from the tasseled Turkish fez, the pillbox is a round,
brimless hat with a flat top. After the Second World War, Spanish
designer Cristóbal Balenciaga created the shape as the perfect comple-

*D*esigner Eric Javits's saucy French sailor hat,
above, bears a closer resemblance to the French beret than to the
English sailor hat. Opposite, his cloche takes on an innocent,
country air when the fabric is straw rather than felt.

ment to his knee-length dresses and suits. The elegant effect of the head
rising on an elongated neck, hair tucked beneath a pillbox, was perhaps
best illustrated by actress Audrey Hepburn in many of the films she
made in the sixties. A minimalist hat, the pillbox was clearly a compro-
mise that signaled the rising importance of the coiffure and the fall of
the hat as essential to the well-groomed woman.

 The Toque. There has hardly been a time when this tall brimless
hat has not been in style. In the mid-nineteenth century, during a surge
of enthusiasm for things Russian, an otherwise quite sensible Victorian
Englishwoman might cloak her shoulders in a braid-trimmed Russian cos-

sack's coat and pop a Persian lamb toque on her head. In a Paris ruled by Napoleon III and the huge crinolined skirt, a tiny toque decorated with a plume, flowers, or a veil light as a breath, as worn by the Empress Eugénie, was de rigueur for every woman. And pre-Raphaelite beauties covered their masses of waves in a snood and topped them with a toque perched above the forehead.

The Picture Hat. Also called the garden hat, the cartwheel, and a hundred other charming names, the picture hat is a perennial favorite. Depending on the tilt of the brim, it can suggest a number of moods. In the late eighteenth century, the big-brimmed hat, immortalized in paintings by Gainsborough, was coquettish, perched sideways on the head. During the same period, in the hands of French portraitist Elisabeth Vigée-Lebrun, it appeared more forthright, the brim turned up in front and pinned with a satin cockade. So outrageous did its dimensions become that one modish lady was moved to remark that her new hat, at twenty-nine and a half inches in diameter, was the same size as her new tea table.

The Sporting Hat. When women went riding, hunting, or flying off in monoplanes, they chose smaller versions of what the men wore. But in the early twentieth century, when the new "sport" of motoring appeared, women resolved the fashion challenge their own way: They enveloped themselves in the long dusters the men were wearing; then they clamped soft-crowned hats with brims big as dinner plates on their heads, poked in hat pins, tied on veils, and were ready to roll.

*The picture hat from Patina is the essence of
sophistication in dove gray straw, its wide grosgrain band studded
with a clutch of snowdrops and a handful of berries.*

*P*atina transforms a plain straw hat with flutings
of ribbon, an antique button, and a cocky feather, above left.
Above right, a straw garden hat piped with covered wire
curlicues is misted with roses of tulle.

The same silhouette alters considerably depending on the fabrics chosen. Though virtually any cloth used in dressmaking ~ silk, leather, velvet, tulle, lamé, for example ~ can be pressed into service on a hat form made of a coarsely woven, stiffened cloth called buckram, felt and straw are among the most popular.

Felt. Felt is one of the oldest fabrics in the world, probably older than woven ones because it was easier to make and certainly less destructible. Two types have been available for centuries. The better quality is made of fur sheared from beavers. The lesser quality is made of wool. In hat-making, a few ounces of the hair or fur are spread by machine over a perforated metal cone, covered with a wet cloth, and dipped into boiling

*The child's straw sailor in shades of rose, above
left, is the creation of Marta Baumiller. Lilacs and violets,
the very essence of spring, nestle on the brim of honeyed
pale straw from Lola, above right.*

water to be shrunk. After shrinking, the cloth is rolled on a table to dry.
This process is repeated until it becomes densely matted, and the cone-
shaped hat body is about three time the size the finished hat will be.
Many milliners buy their hat bodies ready made and block them themselves. The hat body is first sprayed with water to make it more mal-
leable, then gently stretched over the wooden block. The hat body and
block are tied with rope to keep them in place and put in a cool oven to
dry. Afterward, if crown and brim have been made separately, they are
trimmed of excess felt and stitched together. The join is covered with a
ribbon, and the hat is put on a hot metal block to be ironed. Before the
wiring and final stitches are added, the inside of the hat may be brushed

with lacquer sizing to help hold its shape. A final, thicker coat of lacquer is painted on before the finished hat is shipped.

Straw. Woven and braided of the dried stems of cereal grains ~ wheat, oats, rye, and barley ~ or the leaves of coconut and raffia palms, the straw hat has been an inexpensive way to keep cool for a long, long time, and continues coloring our dreams of the country life from which it sprang. The straw hat shielded bare heads in the sunny days of ancient Greece; in this country, it began to be made in post-Revolutionary times, when, desperate for fashion and dismayed at the cost of bonnets imported from Europe, American girls started plaiting the fine and plentiful straw of the fields around them. Today, though such famous straws as the Italian leghorn ~ once synonymous with the picture hat ~ have vanished, straw hats and braid are imported from China and the Philippines, and to a lesser extent from South America and Italy.

Straw hats come in two basic shapes: the hood, a small beehive form, and the capeline, a

Two straws in the wind: A picture hat from Hat Attack, left, boasts a Western dip to its crown and a straw hatband and rim. On the right, Patricia Underwood's open-crown hat is sashed in black grosgrain and filliped with a rose.

A*bove, a tailored gray felt is left free of*
all extras. Left, navy blue taffeta ribbon is crumpled
around the same gray crown, an antique shoe
buckle glitters with paste diamonds, and a tiny tuft
of bluets supplies the final touch.

bell-like shape with a clearly defined brim. The straw is dampened, molded, and sometimes ironed for smoothness on wooden blocks. If the crown and brim have been made and blocked separately, the two parts are invisibly stitched back together.

A third type of hat is one constructed of straw braid chain-stitched round and round from a "button" at the top of the crown. If the brim is to be large, a broad collar is laid on the brim block; and the braid, pinned and stitched in sections, is gradually wound down to the edge. After a hat is completely dry, the inside may be brushed with a straw stiffener and ribbon added to hide the join between crown and brim and to cover the brim's rough edge.

Trim. Though silhouette and fabric are the most important aspects of a hat, the trimmings go far in giving clues to the wearer's manner and mood. A heavy veil, by obscuring the face and its expression, inevitably gives an aura of enigma. A cloche virtually covered in sprays of lily-of-the-valley is certain to seem nothing less than the most lyrical, lighthearted herald of spring. A plume invariably brings a note of boldness and self-possession. Flowers, feathers, veils, jewels, fur, ribbons, bows, beads, and swags of fabric are all basic to the trimmings repertoire. Adorning a hat is a matter of imagination and luck, developing a magpie's eye for the glittering object in an obscure place that will touch a hat with witchcraft. To aid your endeavors, seek the serendipitous ornament ~ in bridal shops, card shops, at a florist's or upholsterer's, or at a fabric counter. Garland a summer straw with twinings of just-picked dark green ivy, fragile fern, or daisies; stitch on pearl or crystal beads that shimmer like dewdrops. In the fall, poke tassels of wheat or dried flowers into a hatband made of rope or raffia. And in winter, spark a felt with holly, mistletoe, silk braid, tassels, loops of velvet studded with an old cameo pin, swags of taffeta.

An appropiate treasure chest for trimmings:
An antique wooden box is filled with old French and
wire-shaped ribbon, thread, and bits of fabric.

OLD TO NEW AND BACK AGAIN

T he most impor-
tant step in enlivening neglected hats ~
and it may be all that is needed for
some ~ is to softly brush or blow away
the dust of forgetfulness (use a cash-
mere brush or hair dryer set on cool).
After, a weary felt, its crown stuffed
with clean rags, can be pressed with
damp cloth and moderate iron, then
given a last fluffing with a suede brush.
A fur, fur felt, or velvet hat can be
quickly steamed and brushed. Old flowers come to life when steamed, their
petals rounded with the fingers; ribbons
can be easily replaced. But if a hat
seems too shiny-new, give it a pinch
and a poke when damp, and garland it
with antique silk or dried flowers, a
faded ribbon pinned with a locket, lace
that has been dipped in tea. And there
you are, a milliner in the grand tradi-
tion, everyone asking how you did it.

III

THE MILLINER'S TRADE

*W*HEN I WAS
SIX I MADE MY MOTHER
A LITTLE HAT ~
OUT OF HER NEW BLOUSE.

Lilly Daché

 n eighteenth-century France, Paris was the center of the universe for a new professional, the milliner. She made fashion tick, changing the basic dress to the confections that led docile husbands to the edge of bankruptcy or, in the case of Louis XVI, over it. It was the milliner whose inventiveness created a seemingly endless array of head coverings, each with its own special name. A hundred years later, the fame of the milliner continued, as great as that of the couturier. Her name was said breathlessly, her creations longed for. Chic Parisiennes, who instinctively understood that a hat can change the appearance of a dress, but a dress cannot change the appearance of a hat, purchased as many hats as they could afford for each ensemble. Today, the legacy of these forceful craftswomen thrives. In California, New York, and centers in between, milliners are turning fantasies into realities. Advisers as well as creators, the milliners guide their clients to new and better perceptions of themselves.

PATINA:

Ardent Traditionalists

L ongtime friends, and collectors of Edwardian furbelows, Katrin Noon, above left, and Jodi Bentson, above right, of Patina Millinery in Los Angeles, finally came to realize they had a need to share their finds and reproduce the mood of one of the most golden hours in the life of hats: the Edwardian era. One of the attractions of the period for the two has always been its fine detailing and craftsmanship, particularly in millinery. From about 1913 to 1918, the hat, which, says Katrin, had been "a major, major statement on top of the head in the Victorian era, became more integrated. You didn't have whole families of birds on top of it."

A whimsical souvenir of the sea is Patina's straw,
opposite, ribboned in coral satin with starfish, sea horses, and
pearls in a beguiling net of golden lace. Above, the open-crown
sunny-day straw is latticed with straw braid.

Today, Katrin and Jodi continue searching, scouting flea markets
and swaps, auctions and the basements of millinery supply houses, as
well as private sources, to find crushed and neglected trims from the
United States and Europe. The best day of the week is the one when
boxes of their discoveries arrive. Then these once-forgotten beauties
find a new place in the sun, stitched on such familiar Edwardian shapes
as the wide-brimmed cloche and the little sailor. If one of the blossoms
is faded, a leaf a bit tattered, a silky petal a little tired, generally no
effort is made to renew it. "We prefer it when the trims are a little
stained, when they've had it," says Katrin. "They have an authentic
look of the time, a patina."

LOLA:

A Passionate Hatmaker

I n her shop in New York City's Flatiron district, surrounded by hats whimsical and serious, Dutch-born Lola Ehrlich is pursuing a lifelong passion. When the passion first struck, she was taking a millinery course in England. After that, it slumbered fitfully until seven years ago, when she threw over a career in another area of fashion, attended night courses at New York's Fashion Institute of Technology, and started her business "on a shoestring." "I had no proof anyone would like my hats," she says. "But the business took off. The time was right." The time continues to be right, and her clientele delights in the hats she concocts. Most of her customers are women "with

*A sampling of Lola's craft, opposite,
illustrates the breadth of her hats: classic but always a little
offbeat. Above, the biggest, floppiest picture hat, in packable
blue denim, makes a perfect sun umbrella.*

a strong visual sense and a strong sense of themselves. They're not traditional businesswomen." For them, a high-crowned hat in watermelon red studded with seeds, a veritable tray of pink roses, or a packable little nothing of pastel tulle is exactly the answer for the life they lead.

In a sense, Lola's hats create themselves; they are what she terms "organic." "I don't sketch first," she remarks. "That limits you. I fiddle with the materials, try this and that. The materials guide me. There's no point in considering a hat as just a decorative object," she says. "I have to understand its meaning. People don't wear clothes the way they did in the fifties and sixties. The hat is no longer part of a uniform. It's an attitude."

ROSEMARY WARREN:

Romantic Individualist

here was never a question about what Rosemary Warren of Rabbit Works would do when she grew up. By the time she was nine, not only was she wearing hats her mother made for her, she was making headdresses herself. She was also totally enthralled by her great-aunt, a millinery model and assistant to New York–based hat designer Mr. John. It was from her that Rosemary received instructions in the careful arts of sewing and embroidery.

Rosemary loves the soft look of vintage hats, left, embellished with whimsical flowers and lush bows. Above is a fairy bride's crown of tiny wands, a ring of roses, and a flounce of net.

After twelve years in her West Hollywood studio overlooking the Santa Monica Mountains, Rosemary continues to take millinery lessons, though now they're lessons from the environment. "Nature's not contrived," she says. "Even when it's wired, a branch goes where it wants to go." She studies her materials ~ the vintage flowers, leaves, and ribbons that litter her worktable ~ before beginning a project. "The things," she explains, "just take over." Today, she searches for hat bodies whose characteristics come as close as possible to the suppleness of the old ones. With that kind of straw, "the hat feels like it's been on your head forever," she says. That's a very desirable state of affairs.

PATRICIA UNDERWOOD:

Master Craftswoman

Her most renowned creations are perhaps those sweeping straws so like the one Katherine Hepburn wore in *The Philadelphia Story*. In fact, they are only one of the many kinds of hats Patricia Underwood has been making for twenty years. If once, as the New York designer herself sees it, her hats reached too hard for fantasy, today, whatever else they may offer the romantic sensibility, they are meant to be practical. Practicality, combined with elegance, simplicity, and

Patricia interprets two fine straws, left. One is naturally honeyed, the other is the color of ripe plums. Above, tools of the trade include a welter of straw hoods, straw braid, and spools of tinted cotton thread.

⊼

subtle color, is fundamental to her design credo. "Modern hats are to do with shape," she says. "In my studio, we try to make adornment an integral part of the hat." For this reason, even the stripes and hatbands of her beautifully balanced soft straws are themselves of straw, not of some new, contrasting material. This pared-down simplicity ensures that nothing will distract the eye of the viewer from the face of the wearer. "A hat has to bring attention to you, as a person," says Patricia. Though she considers the most important requirement for wearing a hat to be confidence, she also believes it can work the other way around. "If a woman wears a hat well, the hat can inspire her with confidence."

THE HATMAKER'S DAUGHTER

W hen you're small, what better way to spend a rainy day than to play dress-up? Lucky little girls have their own special boxes to dig into. Luckiest of all, however, is Lucy Green, a milliner's daughter. If she is good, uses blunt-nosed scissors, and puts things away when she finishes, she may stay in the workroom with her mother, Louise, and make hats, too. For a hat so big she can scarcely peep out from under the brim, she may chose fluffy feathers, cockades, a jeweled pin, bunches of tiny peach satin roses, silvery leaves, or swatches of tulle. Sometimes, even if the weather's fine, Lucy invites some friends in to play. Together, they sit at their own small table heaped with bits of finery, snipping and twining, pinning and prodding, hard at work making hats nearly as beautiful as those that Lucy's mother makes.

IV

CROWNING TOUCHES

HERE IS

NOT SO VARIABLE A THING

IN NATURE AS

A LADY'S HEAD-DRESS.

Joseph Addison

owever exciting, however many people may be there, an occasion is less an occasion without a hat. There should be a chance to glimpse, near at hand or in the distance, a curling of feathers, a twinkle of sequins, the toss of a brim, an insouciance of flowers adrift in a veil, and to answer the sight with a crowning glory of one's own. Without a hat, the occasion hasn't been accorded its due, its potential for fantasy exploited to the fullest. Though today the hat is no longer a symbol of social rank or role, it still distinguishes the occasion. Without a hat, the ceremony is not quite as serious and affecting; without a hat, the fete is simply not as much fun. If there seem to be fewer occasions for hats now than in the past, a moment's reflection suggests that this is a mistaken impression. The occasions are still there: weddings and christenings in the serene stillness of private chapels and sun-dusted churches; bat mitzvahs in the solemnity of temple sanctuaries; engagement teas, bridal showers, school

*Peerless white carries romance on its wings:
Above, the straw hat by Tia Mazza, its folded-back brim softly bowed
in silk, is studded with one exquisite camellia. Opposite, recalling
the delights of a luncheon party in the twenties, are a picture hat, a turban-
spun toque, and a sheer, deep-brimmed horsehair cloche.*

graduations, holidays, weekend dinner parties, summer gatherings and
garden parties beneath white tents. All these occasions become more
graceful yet as friends and acquaintances nod to each other, heads heavy
as full-blown roses with superlative hats. What makes it seem there aren't
as many occasions as there once were is that there is less willingness to
accord these events the distinction they once had. One hundred years
ago, even everyday happenings took on the air of an occasion, each
moment outlined, clear and ceremonial. A stroll in the park, a ride in an
open carriage, punting on the river, weekending in the country, making
the Grand Tour of the Continent ~ nothing was undertaken casually.

The frosting of a lace dress is echoed by a sailor hat
twined in tulle, ivy, and jonquil buds and richly bowed, above, for
the bridesmaid. Opposite: Graduation calls for a deep blue straw
cloche and a modest straw version adorned with velvet petals.

Undoubtedly, this need for ceremony and correctness could be
stifling, but it also seems that the elaboration enriched life. In
Edwardian Daughter, Sonia Keppel, the daughter of the famous English
beauty Alice Keppel, suggests the pleasures that accompanied her family's preparation for holiday trips. For Sonia and her sister, it meant
choosing light dresses and straw hats, with black stockings for the older
girl, white ones for the younger. For their mother, it meant an imposing
array of luggage that filled the hall ~ "the wardrobe trunks standing up
on end and high enough to stand in; hat boxes; shoe boxes; rugs; traveling cushions, her traveling jewel case." An Edwardian lady was bol-

*E*lizabeth Moir used ribbons of pure silk to wreathe
a beret with roses and spring flowers, opposite. Above, a saucer-
brimmed black velour hat from Tia Mazza is swathed with a
chiffon scarf and studded with a single white poppy .

stered by her wardrobe in all her activities; her costume and her hat
were her defenses. She made entrances and exits as if taking part in a
processional, and was as completely turned out ~ hat, gloves, shoes ~
for a stroll in the park as for an evening at the opera. No one ques-
tioned the importance of her attentiveness to these rituals. Hats were
considered so significant that cars were designed with them in mind.
"That year," Colette wrote in her beloved *Gigi*, "fashionable automo-
biles were being built with a slightly higher body and a rather wide top,
to accommodate the exaggerated hats affected by Caroline Otero,
Liane de Pougy, and other conspicuous figures of 1899: and, in conse-
quence, they could sway gently at every turn of the wheel."

*S*uzanne's shop window in New York City,
opposite, overflows with the stuff that wedding dreams are
made of. Perhaps the crowning choice is a comely white hat,
above, enveloped in a gauzy haze of net.

By rejoicing in today's freedom to be carefree, too often we overlook
the pleasure that such ladies had in adding the extra notes to their
wardrobes instead of eliminating them, savoring the unique moment
instead of speeding by it. Our days, too, could be made more notable by
adding flourishes to our occasions; by beginning to plan the minute we cir-
cle a date on the calendar, jot down an engagement in a diary, break the
seal on the heavy envelope holding an invitation, or hear the words "Won't
you join us?" What pleasure in prolonging the preparation for an event by
rushing back to the shop for the hat we can't forget, or the single white
flower that could magically alter a beloved chapeau already in the closet.

For the bride, in addition to designing or commissioning the most wonderful hat she will ever wear, giving full play to the occasion may mean creating hats for her bridesmaids and flower girls as well. Bridal hats have a long history: fuller, more varied, more encompassing than the bridal veil. Even now, veils are most often limited to formal, religious ceremonies, while the hat brings its singular, individual note to numerous other types of weddings: the second marriage, later marriages, civil weddings in judges' chambers, small weddings at home, in the garden, weddings happily spur of the moment.

In one of the bridal hat's most triumphant periods ~ during the nineteenth-century's love affair with the bonnet ~ a bride's blushes were only to be guessed at, concealed by a bonnet that was a shell of silk, velvet, or straw, whose modesty was further underscored by sprigs of orange blossoms or dark-leaved, starry myrtle ~ the ancients' flower of love ~ by loops of ribbon, pristine pleats, fillips of lace, or a sheer lace veil. In the twenties and thirties the garden hat often dominated wedding festiv-

The mother of the bride, a cherished member of the wedding, chooses a serene white straw picture hat, its brim rimmed in contrasting dark ribbon. The creation is all subtle flattery, pinned up on one side with a resplendent bloom.

*The bride above wears a rose-
covered cap rimmed with a flounce of point d'esprit
designed by Victoria DiNardo. Right, a sheer
white straw cartwheel is adorned with a luxurious
outpouring of silk organza petals.*

ities, floating with generous grace around the faces
of the bride, bridal party, and guests.

Today, if the etiquette that once demanded a
hat at a wedding is less stringent, the effect of wearing a hat is just as enchanting. For all the magic of
her dress, it is the bride's face and headdress that
draw and hold all eyes. Her wedding day is her
chance to choose a hat that answers a personal fantasy rather than the dictates of fashion ~ to pick
white, or any of the rainbow's ethereal hues: muted
pink, dove gray, summer sky blue. It is an opportuni-
ty to wear a hat caught in webs of veiling, ringed
with a plunder of flowers from the garden or dark
velvet leaves, a hat sprinkled with silken petals,

shimmering with the tiniest points of light ~ crystal beads, seed pearls, iridescent sequins that touch her head as if with glancing rays of moonlight.

At all moments, public and private, the hat is a wish, a deliberate desire to bring romance into being ~ a brim making a mystery of the eyes; the flattery of a veil softening the contours of the face; a wreath of flowers surrounding the hat's crown like the garlands that circled maidens' heads in classical times. It might be the hat given even more romantic resonance with the scent of fresh flowers and herbs: tiny, pungent chrysanthemums sounding the poignant note of autumn; the powdery-yellow aroma of daisies embodying summer; twists of honeysuckle, sweet roses woven with the silvery tendrils of willow and sprigged with rosemary.

Days or years later, leafing through an album, spying one's photograph, smiling with a mix of shyness and pride from beneath the brim of the favored hat, all the pleasure of that instant will return afresh.

Victoria DiNardo's variation on the nineteenth-century riding hat is whipped round with a flowing point d'esprit veil caught in a white satin bow so fragile even dreams could not have conjured it.

HOW TO
WEAR A HAT

⌖

How to wear a hat? With aplomb, knowing you are absolutely right. Rules are yesterday. How you wear your hair, your size, how you feel at that moment, are what count. Perhaps the only "rule" to consider is that of proportion. A large hat balances a narrow outfit or its opposite, a skirt on the scale of Miss Scarlett's hoopskirt. A small hat is fine with both the narrow and the billowing silhouette. A hat with a brim is worn straight on the head, unless you're under ten.

But you may find, for instance, that if you're small, a big hat isn't wrong: It makes you look devastatingly fragile. If you're tall, a high-crowned hat may only make you more majestic. One of the greatest enemies to hat-wearing is self-consciousness. Stand tall and proud.

Permissions and Credits

꘡

1: Photograph by Thomas Hooper

5: Photograph by Luciana Pampalone

7: Photograph by Beth Ava

8-9: Photograph by Luciana Pampalone

11: Painting by Pierre-Auguste Renoir, French, 1841-1919, *Two Sisters (On the Terrace)*, oil on canvas, 1881, 100.5 x 81 cm, Mr. and Mrs. Lewis Larned Coburn Memorial Collection, 1933.455. Photograph © 1993, The Art Institute of Chicago. All Rights Reserved.

12: Photograph by Michael Skott

13: Photograph by Wendi Schneider

14: Photograph by Toshi Otsuki

15: Photograph by Thomas Hooper

16: Photograph by Michael Dunne

17: Photograph by Toshi Otsuki

18: Photographs by Toshi Otsuki (left), Douglas Foulke (right)

19: Photographs by Toshi Otsuki (left), Thomas Hooper (right)

20-21: Photograph by Star Ockenga

22: Photograph by Starr Ockenga

23: Photograph by Michael Skott

24: Photograph by Wendi Schneider

26-27: Photograph by Scott Dorrance

28-29: Photograph by Luciana Pampalone

31: Painting by Mary Cassat, American, 1845-1926, *Portrait of a Young Woman in Black*, 1883. Baltimore Museum of Art: The Peabody Institute of The City of Baltimore, on indefinite loan to The Baltimore Museum of Art, BMA L.1964.18.

32: Photograph by Carol Ford

33: Photograph by Carol Ford

34: Photograph by Wendi Schneider

36: Photograph by Wendi Schneider

37: Photograph by Toshi Otsuki

38: Photograph by Luciana Pampalone

39: Photograph by Thomas Hooper

40: Photograph by Thomas Hooper

42: Photographs by Thomas Hooper (left), Wendi Schneider (right)

43: Photographs by Toshi Otsuki (left),
Luciana Pampalone (right)

44: Photograph by Toshi Otsuki

46: Photograph by Toshi Otsuki

47: Photograph by Toshi Otsuki

48: Photograph by Tina Mucci

50-51: Photograph by Carin Krasner

52-53: Photograph by Luciana Pampalone

55: Painting by Edgar Degas, French,
1834-1917, *The Millinery Shop*, oil on canvas, 1879-84, 100 x 110.7 cm, Mr. and
Mrs. Lewis Larned Coburn Memorial
Collection, 1933.28. Photograph © 1993,
The Art Institute of Chicago. All Rights
Reserved.

56: Photograph by Ken Merfeld

57: Photograph by Ken Merfeld

58: Photograph by Thomas Hooper

59: Photograph by Thomas Hooper

60: Photograph by Toshi Otsuki

61: Photograph by Pierre Chanteau

62: Photograph by Pierre Chanteau

63: Photograph by Toshi Otsuki

64: Photograph by Carin Krasner

65: Photograph by J. Samuelson

66: Photograph by Carin Krasner

67: Photograph by Carin Krasner

68: Photograph by Luciana Pampalone

69: Photograph by Luciana Pampalone

70: Photograph by Luciana Pampalone

71: Photograph by Luciana Pampalone

72-73: Photograph by Elyse Lewin

74-75: Photograph by Toshi Otsuki

77: Painting by Mary Cassat, American,
1845-1926, *The Cup of Tea*, 1879.
Copyright © 1983 By The Metropolitan
Museum of Art.

78: Photograph by Toshi Otsuki

79: Photograph by Toshi Otsuki

80: Photograph by Luciana Pampalone

81: Photograph by Toshi Otsuki

82: Photograph by Toshi Otsuki

83: Photograph by Toshi Otsuki

84: Photograph by Toshi Otsuki

85: Photograph by Toshi Otsuki

86: Photograph by Toshi Otsuki

88: Photograph by Toshi Otsuki

89: Photograph by Nancy Johnson

91: Photograph by Toshi Otsuki

92-93: Photograph by Beth Ava

96: Photograph by William P. Steele